Contents

* These pieces are compatible with *Cello Time*.

2. Under arrest!

Four short crot - chets

played on G, (rest) one fell off and left just three. (rest)

1 2 3, (rest) 1 2 3, (rest) one fell off and left just three. (rest)

Printed in Great Britain

OXFORD UNIVERSITY PRESS, MUSIC DEPARTMENT, GREAT CLARENDON STREET, OXFORD OX2 6DP

OXFORD

Joggers Piano Book
Fiddle Time and Viola Time

Kathy and David Blackwell

OXFORD
UNIVERSITY PRESS

Great Clarendon Street, Oxford OX2 6DP, England
198 Madison Avenue, New York, NY10016, USA

Oxford is a registered trade mark of Oxford University Press
in the UK and in certain other countries

3 5 7 9 10 8 6 4

ISBN 978–0–19–322119–2

Music and text origination by
Barnes Music Engraving Ltd., East Sussex
Printed in Great Britain on acid-free paper by
Caligraving Limited, Thetford, Norfolk.

Teacher's note

This book contains all the piano accompaniments required for both *Fiddle Time* and *Viola Time*
Joggers. Pieces are labelled with the relevant instruments, as 'Violin/Viola', 'Violin', or 'Viola'.
Different parts for violin and viola are shown with separate stemming. In addition, a number of
pieces are compatible with pieces in *Cello Time Joggers*, and these are marked with an asterisk
on the Contents page.

4. Down up

Down,   up,   E   string,   down,   up,   A   string,

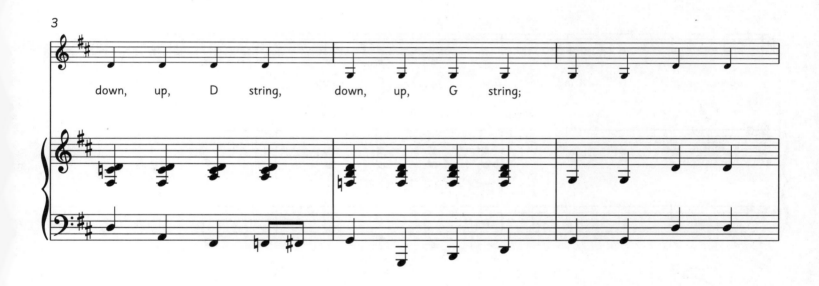

down,   up,   D   string,   down,   up,   G   string;

Play   the   A   and   end   with   D.

4. Down up

Down,   up,   A   string,   down,   up,   D   string,

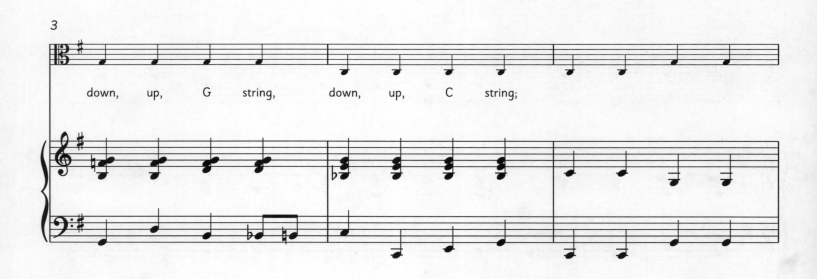

down,   up,   G   string,   down,   up,   C   string;

Play   the   D   and   end   with   G.

7. Fast lane

8. In flight

9. Lift off!

10. Katie's waltz

12. Tap dancer

13. Rhythm fever

14. Here it comes!

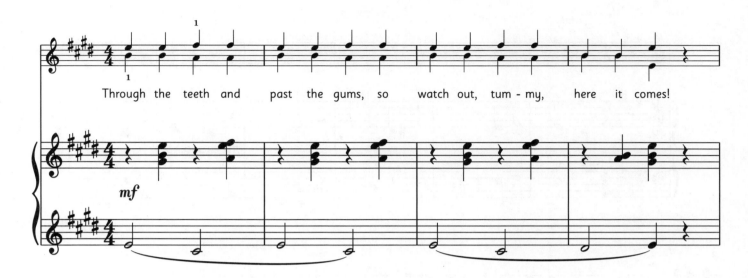

Through the teeth and past the gums, so watch out, tum - my, here it comes!

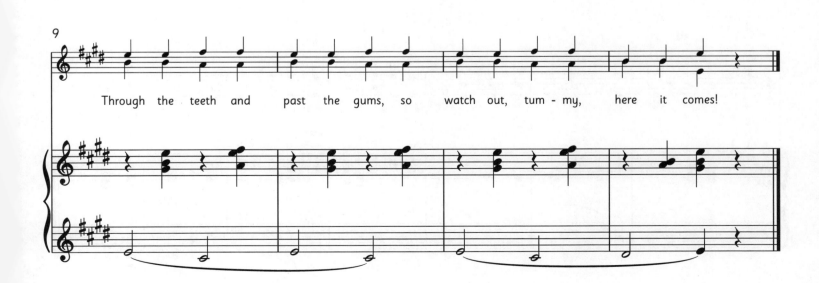

Through the teeth and past the gums, so watch out, tum - my, here it comes!

15. So there!

16. Rowing boat

18. Tiptoe, boo!

Spookily!

Tip - toe   tip - toe   tip - toe, boo! (etc.)

p staccato

19. Travellin' slow

20. Lazy cowboy

20. C string boogie

* Turn around or, if you are sitting, stand up and sit down again!

22. Clare's song
next page

23. City lights

Nos. 22 and 23 are reversed to avoid a page turn.

22. Clare's song

24. The three friends

(Violin duet with viola ensemble part)

Finnish

24. Daydream

25. Chinese garden

25. On the prowl

26. Summer sun

28. Ready, steady, go now!

30. Happy go lucky (for Iain)

33. Listen to the rhythm

Lis - ten to the rhy - thm on my vi - o - lin.
vi - o - la.
stacc.

Crot - chets sound like this:
Quar - ter - notes like this:

Crot - chets sound like that!
Quar - ter - notes like that!
Lis - ten to the rhy - thm on my

34. Cattle ranch blues

35. In the groove

35. In the groove

36. Stamping dance

Czech.

37. Distant bells

38. Lazy scale

39. The old castle

With a singing tone

Con ped.

rit.

39. Runaway train

The music is written out in full in the viola part.

40. Rocking horse

41. Patrick's reel

42. Calypso time

42. Calypso time

43. Knock, knock!

'Knock, knock.' 'Who's there?'   'Cook.'   'Cook who?'   'That's the first cuc - koo I've

heard this year!'   'Knock, knock.' 'Who's there?'   'Jes - ter.'   'Jes - ter who?'

'Jes - ter min-ute, I'll un - lock the door!'

43. Tudor tune

45. Carrion crow

(Violin duet with viola ensemble part)

American

46. Flying high

46. Flying high

47. Fiddle Time

47. Viola Time

Joggers Piano Book

Fiddle Time and Viola Time

Fiddle Time and *Viola Time* are compatible series for young violinists and viola players. Packed with lively original tunes, well-known pieces, and easy duets, they are carefully paced and organized to build confidence every step of the way.

   Joggers Piano Book brings together in one volume all of the piano accompaniments for **Fiddle Time Joggers** and *Viola Time Joggers*. Each accompaniment is labelled with the relevant instruments, and differences between the violin and viola melodies are indicated clearly throughout. Fingering and bowing for both instruments are also included.

Fiddle Time and *Viola Time*
by Kathy and David Blackwell

Fiddle Time Starters (a beginner book for the young violinist)	violin book
Fiddle Time Joggers (a first book of very easy pieces)	violin book and CD piano accompaniment book
Fiddle Time Runners (a second book of easy pieces)	violin book and CD piano accompaniment book
Fiddle Time Sprinters (a third book of pieces)	violin book and CD piano accompaniment book
Fiddle Time Scales 1 (pieces, puzzles, scales, and arpeggios)	violin book
Fiddle Time Scales 2 (musicianship and technique through scales)	violin book
Fiddle Time Christmas (a stockingful of 32 easy pieces)	violin book
Viola Time Joggers (a first book of very easy pieces)	viola book and CD piano accompaniment book
Viola Time Runners (a second book of easy pieces)	viola book and CD piano accompaniment book

OXFORD
UNIVERSITY PRESS

www.oup.com

ISBN 0-19-322119-5

9 780193 221192